THE BIG BITE
BOOK OF
BARBECUES

THE BIG BITE BOOK OF BARBECUES

MEG JANSZ

SMITHMARK

This edition published in 1995 by
SMITHMARK Publishers Inc.,
16 East 32nd Street,
New York, NY 10016.

1 2 3 4 5 6 7 8 9

SMITHMARK books are available for bulk purchase
for sales promotion and premium use. For details
write or call the manager of special sales,
SMITHMARK Publishers Inc.,
16 East 32nd Street, New York,
NY 10016; (212) 532-6600

ISBN 0-8317-0758-5

Printed in Singapore

CREDITS

Author and home economist: Meg Jansz
Home economist's assistant: Lucy Pitcairn-Knowles
Managing editor: Lisa Dyer
Photographer: Ken Field
Designer: Ian Sandom
Stylist: Marian Price
Filmset: SX Composing Ltd, England
Color Separation: P&W Graphics Pte, Ltd,
   Singapore

Other titles of interest:
The Big Bite Book of BURGERS
The Big Bite Book of PIZZAS
The Big Bite Book of SALADS

CONTENTS

INTRODUCTION

The Big Bite Book of Barbecues contains a delicious selection of varied recipes to suit all tastes and occasions. Contrary to the popular belief that barbecues cater primarily for the meat-eater, barbecuing is evolving fast to suit all contemporary tastes. The recipes in the book demonstrate the versatility of barbecuing, with an entire chapter devoted to imaginative vegetable-based dishes.

Historically, barbecuing was the original style of cooking, with our ancestors of centuries ago spit-roasting whole animals over live coals. In more recent times, the art of barbecuing has evolved to become, in modern societies, a popular way of eating "al fresco."

CHARCOAL OR WOOD GRILLS

Whether they are permanent features, made from a brick base, or portable, most grills are designed for just grilling food. They consist of a firebox that holds the fuel and an adjustable rack, which enables you to place food at different heights above the fuel.

There are two types of coal fuel that can be used: lumpwood charcoal is cheaper, easier to light and burns hotter than its alternative, pressed briquettes. However, once briquettes have been lit they last a lot longer.

Fire starters or lighter fluid are also essential to start the grill. Fire starters should be placed in the bottom of the firebox, and a 3-inch pyramid of charcoal constructed over the top. The fire starters are then ignited with a taper to start the fire. Use lighter fluid to help the fire, if necessary.

Once the grill is lit, it can take up to one hour to reach the "ashen coal or wood stage," which means it is ready to cook on. Please remember to follow the manufacturer's instructions carefully if you are using lighter fluid. Make sure the hot coals are spread out evenly. To maintain the heat, gradually add fresh coal around the outer edges.

Wood can also be used as a fuel, but is more difficult to start. If you use wood, use hardwoods which burn longer. Let the flames die right down before cooking. Wood barbecues will take 30-45 minutes to reach the point where they are ready for cooking.

Aromatic wood chips are available for use on barbecues to impart flavors to the food. Oak and hickory wood chips are especially popular and there are also more unusual ones, like mesquite and cherry. Wood chips should be soaked for about 30 minutes in cold water, then drained and placed on the ashen coals.

GAS GRILLS

These grills only need 5 or 10 minutes to heat and the temperature can be easily controlled. Gas grills either have vaporizer bars or lava rocks that are heated up by gas burners. The cooking rack is set above these. Moisture drips from the cooking food onto the bars and vaporizes to give the food an aromatic smoked flavor. Pre-soaked wood chips can also be placed in a foil container on the vaporizer bar, or on the heated lava rocks, but do not put food too near the container.

RIGHT: Fish, seafood, vegetables, meat and even certain cheeses barbecue well, and you may want to try the Mushroom & Mozzarella Brochettes (see page 64), pictured here.

GENERAL SAFETY

Always place the grill on even ground and away from trees, buildings or fences. Once the grill is alight, do not leave it unattended, and keep children away from it.

Let embers cool completely before disposing. They will take several hours to cool. Allow transportable grills to cool completely before packing them away. Always use long-handled tongs when handling food on the grill. Never use gasoline or similar flammable liquids to light a grill and keep matches well away from the grill. Have a bottle of water handy to douse the flames if they become too unruly.

FOOD SAFETY AND COOKING

Keep raw food out of the sun. Make sure that pieces of meat are well cooked. Adequate lighting around a grill is essential at night to check whether food is properly cooked. Never cook frozen food on a grill – it must always be thoroughly defrosted first.

All the recipes should be cooked over a medium-hot grill, unless otherwise indicated. Barbecuing is a rather unpredictable cooking method, and you will need to adjust the cooking times according to the intensity of your grill. If you find the coals are becoming too hot, simply raise the grill rack to the next setting on your grill.

EQUIPMENT

There is a large array of barbecue equipment for sale these days, but there are a few essential pieces. Wear an apron to prevent splatters on clothes and use well-padded oven mitts to handle hot metal skewers and griddle pans or plates. Long-handled tongs, a fork and a metal spatula are essential for turning food. Use

metal skewers for robust food, oiling them first. Wood skewers should be used for delicate foods. Soak them in cold water before use to prevent them catching fire. When barbecuing food in foil packages, use heavy-duty foil.

A wide range of hinged wire baskets are available for barbecuing. These are especially useful for fish and fragile food. Metal griddle pans or plates that can be heated on the grill are useful for cooking fragile foods that would otherwise be tricky to cook on a grill. Always oil the heated griddle before placing food on it. A stiff wire brush is essential for brushing down the grill bars after use, and use a metal scraper for removing any burnt food.

MARINADES

Marinating plays a vital part in barbecuing, as it adds extra depth of flavor. Fish and shellfish generally require a shorter marinating time than meat. If food has been marinated in the refrigerator, allow it to come back to room temperature before cooking.

Marinades that contain acidic elements, like vinegar or citrus juice, will tenderize the food. Oils in marinades help prevent food from sticking, and herbs and spices create mouth-watering flavors. All in all, marinating can turn the simplest cut of meat or piece of fish, or vegetable, into something more special.

Barbecuing should be an enjoyable way of cooking, so do not rush. Above all, relax, enjoy this sociable way of cooking and eating, and savor the tantalizing aromas and tastes that barbecuing produces.

RIGHT: Using marinades to brush meat and vegetables while barbecuing adds extra flavor.

QUICK BARBECUES

A range of "fuss-free" recipes are included in this chapter, all which take a minimum of time to prepare and would be suitable for impromptu summer meals or weekday family meals. Although certain recipes, such as Spare Ribs with Tangy BBQ Sauce and Horseradish Steaks, benefit from being marinated for several hours before cooking, as this provides a better depth of flavor, the end result will still be tasty if you do not have the time to marinate.

TERIYAKI RIBS

3 pounds meaty pork spare ribs
Salad and crusty bread, to serve (optional)

MARINADE
6 tablespoons clear honey
3 tablespoons dark soy sauce
6 tablespoons tomato ketchup
1½ teaspoons cracked black pepper
2 teaspoons Chinese five-spice powder
Grated zest and juice of 1 large orange

Mix the marinade ingredients together in a bowl. Place the spare ribs in a large glass dish and pour the marinade over them. Turn the ribs to coat evenly. Cover and refrigerate for 2-3 hours, if time permits.

Remove the ribs from the marinade, reserving the marinade for basting. Cook the ribs on a prepared grill for about 20 minutes, basting frequently. Serve with salad and crusty bread, if desired.   SERVES 4-6

SPARE RIBS WITH TANGY BBQ SAUCE

3 pounds meaty pork spare ribs

TANGY BBQ SAUCE
2 cloves garlic, crushed
6 tablespoons clear honey
2 tablespoons tomato paste
2 tablespoons chili sauce
2 tablespoons Worcestershire sauce
2 tablespoons soy sauce
4 teaspoons yellow mustard
Juice of 1 lemon

Mix the sauce ingredients together in a bowl. Place the spare ribs in a large glass dish and pour the sauce over the ribs, turning the ribs to coat evenly. Cover and refrigerate for 2 hours, if time permits.

Remove ribs from the grill sauce and pour the remaining sauce into a small saucepan. Cook the ribs on a prepared grill for about 20 minutes, turning frequently. Just before serving, reheat the sauce. Bring the sauce to a boil and boil rapidly for 2-3 minutes. Serve the ribs hot, passing the sauce separately.

SERVES 4-6

RIGHT: Teriyaki Ribs

HORSERADISH STEAKS WITH BBQ VEGETABLES

4 sirloin steaks, weighing about 5 ounces each

MARINADE
1 tablespoon grated horseradish
2 tablespoons cracked black pepper
4 tablespoons vegetable oil
Pinch of salt

HORSERADISH SAUCE
4 tablespoons sour cream
1 teaspoon grated horseradish
Salt and ground black pepper

BBQ VEGETABLES
4 medium zucchini, halved lengthwise
2 red bell peppers, cored, seeded and quartered
4 shallots, unpeeled and halved
Salt and ground black pepper
Oil for brushing

Mix the marinade ingredients together in a bowl. Place the steaks in a shallow glass dish and pour the marinade over. Turn the steaks to coat evenly, cover, and refrigerate for 2 hours.

Mix the sauce ingredients together in a bowl, cover, and refrigerate until required.

Season the vegetables and brush them liberally with oil. Cook them on a prepared grill, turning occasionally and basting with oil. The zucchini require about 12 minutes to cook, the bell peppers 10 minutes, and the shallots 8 minutes. Keep all the vegetables warm while cooking the steaks.

Cook the steaks on the grill, brushing them occasionally with the marinade. For a medium-cooked steak, cook for 3 minutes on each side. Decrease or increase the cooking time if a rare or well-done steak is required. Serve the steaks hot with the Horseradish Sauce and the vegetables. SERVES 4

COFFEE BEAN & MOLASSES RIBS

3 pounds pork spare ribs
3 tablespoons molasses
4 tablespoons vegetable oil
½ cup coarsely ground coffee beans
Salad and baked potatoes, to serve (optional)

Place the spare ribs in a large glass dish. Mix the molasses, oil and coffee beans together in a bowl, and pour over the ribs, turning the ribs to coat evenly. Cover and refrigerate for 2-3 hours, if time permits.

Remove the ribs from the dish, reserving any remaining mixture for basting. Cook the ribs on a prepared grill for about 20 minutes, turning and basting them frequently. Serve with salad and baked potatoes, if desired. SERVES 4-6

TOP: Coffee Bean & Molasses Ribs
BOTTOM: Horseradish Steak with BBQ Vegetables

LIVER & BACON BROCHETTES WITH GRILLED RED ONION

I pound lamb's liver
16 slices bacon
8 wooden or metal skewers
4 tablespoons chopped fresh sage
6 tablespoons olive oil
Sea salt and ground black pepper
4 small red onions, unpeeled and halved
Salad and potatoes, to serve (optional)

Cut the lamb's liver into fairly large chunks. Roll up each slice of bacon. Thread the liver chunks and two bacon rolls onto each skewer.

Mix together the sage and oil, season, and brush the oil all over the prepared brochettes and the halved onions. Cook the onions on a prepared grill for about 8 minutes on each side, brushing occasionally with the sage oil.

Cook the liver and bacon brochettes on the grill for 4-5 minutes on each side, brushing frequently with the sage oil. Serve at once with salad and potatoes, if desired. SERVES 4

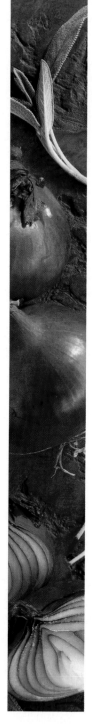

LAMB CHOPS WITH GARLIC, LEMON & OREGANO

4 cloves garlic
4 teaspoons chopped fresh oregano
Grated zest and juice of 2 small lemons
4 tablespoons sunflower oil
Sea salt and ground black pepper
8 lamb chops

Preheat an oven broiler to hot. Place the garlic cloves under the broiler for 8-10 minutes, turning them occasionally, until the skins are charred and the garlic cloves feel soft. Squeeze the roasted garlic out of its skin into a bowl, and mash to a paste. Add the oregano, lemon zest and juice, oil and seasoning. Mix well to combine thoroughly.

Place the lamb chops in a shallow bowl and pour the roasted garlic mixture over. Cover and refrigerate for 2 hours, if time permits.

Remove the chops from the garlic mixture, reserving the remaining mixture. Cook the chops on a prepared grill for about 5 minutes on each side. Just before serving, heat up the reserved garlic mixture in a small saucepan and pour it over the barbecued chops. Serve at once. SERVES 4

RIGHT: Liver & Bacon Brochettes with Grilled Red Onion

BEEF & BEAN BURGERS

I pound ground beef
1¼ cups canned red kidney beans, drained
and chopped
I small onion, finely chopped
2 cloves garlic, crushed
I teaspoon chili powder
Salt and ground black pepper
A little oil for brushing
Crisp green lettuce leaves
4 thick slices avocado
I red onion, sliced
4 tablespoons cilantro leaves
4 flour tortillas, warmed
4 tablespoons sour cream
Pickled Mexican chilies, to serve

Place the beef, beans, onion, garlic, chili powder, and salt and pepper in a bowl. Mix well to combine. Divide the mixture into four and shape into equal-sized patties. Refrigerate until required.

Just before cooking, brush each burger with a little oil. Cook on a prepared grill for about 6 minutes on each side for a medium-cooked burger. Decrease or increase the cooking time for either a rare or well-done burger.

Divide the lettuce, avocado, sliced onion and cilantro between the tortillas. Top each with a burger and spoon some sour cream on each one. Serve the burgers with pickled chilies.   SERVES 4

CALIFORNIA DOGS

4 large frankfurters
4 plain or whole-wheat hot dog buns,
split lengthwise
A little softened butter
6 Romaine lettuce leaves, torn into bite-size pieces
4 small tomatoes, sliced
I small onion, sliced

CORN SALSA

I cup canned corn kernels, drained
¼ green bell pepper, finely diced
4 radishes, thinly sliced
½ red onion, finely diced
I clove garlic, crushed
Juice of ½ lemon
I tablespoon chopped fresh parsley
Salt and ground black pepper

Place the ingredients for the salsa in a bowl and mix together gently to combine. Cover and refrigerate.

Make several diagonal slashes in each frankfurter and cook them on a prepared grill for 4 minutes on each side. Place the hot dog buns, cut-side down, on the grill to toast them lightly. Spread a little softened butter on the rolls.

Divide the lettuce, tomato and onion between the four buns, and top each with a frankfurter. Serve them at once with the Corn Salsa.   SERVES 4

TOP: California Dog
BOTTOM: Beef & Bean Burger

MEDITERRANEAN CHARGRILLED SARDINES

The sardines in this recipe are cooked on pairs of skewers, but you could also use a wire fish basket or rack that holds 6 or 12 sardines. If sardines are unavailable, substitute small red snapper and increase the cooking time.

12 sardines
12 small lemon zest strips
12 small rosemary sprigs
8 long bamboo skewers, soaked in cold water for 2 hours
4 lemon wedges

HERB AND LEMON OIL

4 tablespoons extra virgin olive oil
2 teaspoons grated lemon zest
Juice of 1 lemon
1 tablespoon chopped fresh rosemary
1 tablespoon chopped fresh thyme
Salt and ground black pepper

Using a pair of small scissors, slit the bellies of the sardines and discard the guts. Wash the sardines and dry them on paper towels. Stuff a small strip of lemon zest and a rosemary sprig into the cavity of each sardine.

Thread three sardines onto each pair of skewers by pushing one skewer through a sardine just below the head and pushing the second skewer in just above the tail. Thread on the other two sardines in the same way, then repeat the process with the remaining sardines and skewers.

Mix the ingredients for the herb oil together, and brush liberally over the sardines. Cook the sardines on a prepared, very hot grill for 3-4 minutes on each side, basting with more oil while they are cooking.

Slide the cooked sardines off the skewers and serve at once with lemon wedges.   SERVES 4

SALMON WITH CAPERS & GAZPACHO SALSA

4 salmon steaks, weighing about 4 ounces each

MARINADE

3 tablespoons olive oil
Zest and juice of 1 lime
1 tablespoon capers in brine, drained
Pinch of sea salt

GAZPACHO SALSA

4 small tomatoes, peeled, seeded and diced
1 cup diced cucumber
½ onion, diced
½ red bell pepper, diced
1 tablespoon chopped fresh parsley
4 teaspoons chopped fresh cilantro
1 teaspoon superfine sugar
2 tablespoons red wine vinegar
Salt and ground black pepper

Mix the marinade ingredients together in a bowl. Place the salmon steaks in a shallow dish and pour the marinade over. Cover and refrigerate the salmon for 2 hours, if time permits.

Place the ingredients for the salsa in a bowl and mix together gently to combine. Cover and refrigerate until required.

Remove the salmon steaks from the marinade and press a few capers into the flesh of each piece of salmon. Reserve the remaining marinade for basting. Cook the salmon on a prepared grill for 4-5 minutes on each side, turning the fish once and basting occasionally. Serve the salmon hot with the salsa.

SERVES 4

TOP: Mediterranean Chargrilled Sardines
BOTTOM: Salmon with Capers & Gazpacho Salsa

GRILLED TUNA WITH TOMATO & OLIVE SALSA

4 tuna steaks, weighing about 5 ounces each

OLIVE MARINADE

4 tablespoons green olive puree
½ cup olive oil
3 cloves garlic, crushed
Salt and ground black pepper

TOMATO AND OLIVE SALSA

15 black olives, pitted and sliced
4 tomatoes, peeled, seeded and sliced
½ cup sliced sun-dried tomatoes
4 scallions, sliced
14 basil leaves, torn
Pinch of sugar

Mix the marinade ingredients together in a large shallow dish. Add the tuna steaks, turning to coat evenly. Cover and refrigerate for 2 hours, if time permits.

Make the salsa by combining all the ingredients together. Refrigerate until required.

Remove the tuna steaks from the marinade, reserving the marinade for basting. Cook the steaks on a prepared grill for about 5 minutes on each side, basting occasionally. Serve the grilled tuna steaks at once with the salsa. SERVES 4

MESQUITE-SMOKED FISH

Use a solid-fleshed fish for this recipe, such as catfish or angler fish

4 pieces catfish or angler fish tail with the bone, weighing about 7 ounces each
About 1 cup mesquite chips, soaked in cold water for 1 hour
Skewered New Potatoes, to serve (see page 74)

MARINADE

½ cup extra virgin olive oil
4 tablespoons white wine vinegar
4 cloves garlic, crushed
2 teaspoons crushed mixed peppercorns
2 teaspoons chopped Florence fennel fronds (optional)
A little sea salt

Mix the marinade ingredients together in a bowl. Place the fish portions in a shallow dish and pour the marinade over, turning the fish to coat evenly. Cover and refrigerate for 2 hours, if time permits.

Drain the soaked mesquite chips and scatter them over the hot coals of a prepared grill. Remove the fish from the marinade, reserving the marinade for basting. Cook the fish on the grill for about 15 minutes, or until cooked through, turning and basting occasionally. Serve at once with some Skewered New Potatoes, if desired. SERVES 4

RIGHT: Grilled Tuna with Tomato & Olive Salsa

JUMBO SHRIMP WITH CILANTRO MAYONNAISE

16 raw jumbo shrimp in their shells
4 wooden or metal skewers

MARINADE
½ cup sweet chili sauce
4 tablespoons tomato paste
4 teaspoons lemon juice
4 cloves garlic, crushed
4 teaspoons sesame oil

CILANTRO MAYONNAISE
6 tablespoons mayonnaise
½ fresh red chili, seeded and finely chopped
½ small red onion, finely chopped
2 tablespoons chopped fresh cilantro
2 tablespoons lemon juice
Salt and ground black pepper

Mix the marinade ingredients together in a bowl. Add the shrimp to the marinade and toss to coat evenly. Cover and refrigerate for 2 hours, if time permits.

Mix the mayonnaise ingredients together, cover, and refrigerate until required.

Thread four shrimp onto each skewer and cook them on a prepared grill for 4-5 minutes on each side, turning them once. To serve, remove shrimp from skewers, if preferred, and serve with the Cilantro Mayonnaise.　　　SERVES 2

CHARGRILLED LOBSTER WITH HERB BUTTER

Ask your fish dealer to split the lobsters in half, ready for the grill. Otherwise, kill each lobster by piercing with a knife at the central point where the head meets the body. Halve the head, and split in half along the body.

2 raw lobsters, each weighing about 1 pound, split in half lengthwise with claws cracked
Salt and ground black pepper

HERB BUTTER
3 tablespoons softened butter
1 tablespoon chopped fresh chervil
1 teaspoon snipped fresh chives
1 teaspoon finely chopped shallot
Squeeze of lemon juice
Salt and ground black pepper

Place the ingredients for the Herb Butter in a bowl and beat together to combine. Place the flavored butter in an oblong shape on a piece of parchment paper or plastic wrap. Roll up the butter to produce a cylinder, and refrigerate to harden the butter.

Season the lobster flesh lightly with salt and pepper. Cook the lobster halves, cut-side down, on a prepared grill for 8-10 minutes, until the flesh has become opaque and the shells have turned orange.

Cook the claws separately. They are cooked when the shells have turned bright orange. Serve the freshly grilled lobster with discs of Herb Butter.　SERVES 2

TOP: Chargrilled Lobster with Herb Butter
BOTTOM: Jumbo Shrimp with Cilantro Mayonnaise

SPICY & EXOTIC BARBECUES

Influenced by the cuisines of Mexico, the Mediterranean and the Far East, the recipes in this chapter are robustly flavored. Chilies, cilantro, ginger, lime and sesame are ingredients that feature predominantly in the recipes. An exciting selection of chicken, meat, fish and seafood dishes are included, from the spicy Turmeric Shrimp & Pineapple Skewers to the unusual Halibut Chargrilled in Banana Leaves.

MUSTARD-GLAZED CHICKEN DRUMSTICKS

8 chicken drumsticks

MUSTARD MARINADE
2 tablespoons clear honey
2 teaspoons English mustard
2 teaspoons coarse-grain mustard
2 teaspoons Worcestershire sauce
Juice of 1 orange
2 cloves garlic, crushed
½ onion, very finely chopped

Make several deep slashes through the skin of each drumstick and place the chicken in a shallow glass dish.

Mix the marinade ingredients together and pour over the drumsticks. Turn the drumsticks so they are evenly coated in marinade. Cover and refrigerate for 2-3 hours or overnight.

Remove the drumsticks from the marinade, reserving the marinade for basting, and cook the chicken on a prepared grill for about 20 minutes, turning occasionally and basting during cooking. To test that the chicken is cooked, pierce the flesh with a skewer. If the juices run clear, the chicken is ready to serve.

SERVES 4

BARBECUED CHICKEN WITH CHILI & LIME

6 boneless chicken breasts

MARINADE
4 teaspoons chili oil
2 tablespoons clear honey
4 tablespoons chopped fresh cilantro
2 cloves garlic, crushed
Grated zest and juice of 2 limes

CILANTRO AND CHILI YOGURT
½ cup Greek yogurt
½ teaspoon chili oil
Grated zest and juice of 1 lime
4 tablespoons chopped fresh cilantro
1 small fresh red chili, seeded and finely chopped
A little salt

Place the marinade ingredients in a shallow glass dish and mix well to combine. With a sharp knife, make several deep slashes in each chicken and place the chicken breasts in the marinade, turning to coat well. Cover and refrigerate for 3-4 hours.

Mix the yogurt ingredients together in a bowl. Cover and refrigerate until required.

Remove the chicken from the marinade, reserving the marinade for basting. Place the chicken, skin-side up, on a prepared, medium-hot grill. Cook the chicken breasts for 10 minutes, brushing occasionally with the marinade, then turn over and cook for a further 10 minutes. To test if the chicken is cooked, pierce the thickest part of the breast with a skewer. If the juices are still pink, cook until the juices run clear. Serve at once with the yogurt.

SERVES 6

RIGHT: Barbecued Chicken with Chili & Lime

MEXICAN FISH KABOBS

1¼ pounds red snapper fillets, cut into chunks
4 mini red bell peppers, halved, or 8 pickled
cherry peppers
2 onions, cut into 8 wedges each
8 wooden or metal skewers
Spicy Rice, to serve (see page 72)

MARINADE
4 tablespoons chopped fresh cilantro
4 tablespoons olive oil
Juice of 3 limes
4 teaspoons paprika
1 fresh red chili, seeded and finely chopped

GUACAMOLE
2 avocados
Juice of 1 large lime
½ onion, finely chopped
6 tablespoons torn cilantro leaves
Salt and ground black pepper

Place the marinade ingredients in a shallow glass bowl and mix well to combine. Add the chunks of fish and turn to coat evenly. Cover and refrigerate for 2 hours.

Make the Guacamole. Mash the avocados with the lime juice. Stir in the other ingredients, taste and adjust seasoning, and refrigerate until required.

Thread the marinated fish onto the skewers, alternating with the peppers and onion wedges. Reserve the marinade for basting. Cook the kabobs on a prepared grill for about 10 minutes, turning and brushing them with the reserved marinade. Serve at once with the Guacamole and Spicy Rice.   SERVES 4

HALIBUT CHARGRILLED IN BANANA LEAVES

Galangal is used in this recipe for its exotic taste, but you can substitute fresh ginger root. Heavy-duty foil can also be substituted for the banana leaves, but the foil will not need to be oiled.

1-pound piece skinless, boneless halibut, cut into
1-inch cubes
4 pieces banana leaf, about 12 inches square
Oil for brushing
Small wooden skewers

SPICY PASTE
1 large dried red chili
2-inch piece galangal, peeled and chopped
2 stalks lemon grass, finely chopped
2 cloves garlic, crushed
1 shallot, finely chopped
2 lime leaves, finely chopped
1 tablespoon Thai fish sauce
3 tablespoons peanut oil

Prepare the Spicy Paste. Soak the red chili in hot water for 10 minutes, then drain and chop finely. Place the chili and the remaining ingredients in a spice grinder or food processor and blend to a smooth paste.

Transfer the paste to a shallow glass dish, add the cubed fish, and toss the fish to coat evenly. Cover and refrigerate for 2 hours.

Brush the banana leaves with a little oil and divide the marinated fish between them. Wrap up to form packages and secure with wooden skewers. Brush the outside of the leaves with a little oil and cook the packages on a prepared grill for about 10 minutes, until the fish is cooked through.   SERVES 4

TOP: Halibut Chargrilled in Banana Leaves
BOTTOM: Mexican Fish Kabobs

SCALLOP BROCHETTES WITH GINGER & ORANGE

16 large scallops
4 long strips of orange zest
12 ounces zucchini, cut into 12 chunks
4 metal skewers

MARINADE
Juice of 2 oranges
4 teaspoons grated fresh ginger root
4 tablespoons vegetable oil
4 scallions, finely chopped
2 cloves garlic, crushed
Salt and ground black pepper

GINGER AND ORANGE BUTTER
½ cup softened butter
1 tablespoon grated fresh ginger root
1 tablespoon grated orange zest
1 tablespoon orange juice
Salt and ground black pepper

Mix the marinade ingredients together in a large, shallow bowl. Add the scallops to the marinade and turn to coat evenly. Cover and refrigerate for 2 hours.

Mix the ingredients for the butter together and place the butter in an oblong shape on a piece of parchment paper or plastic wrap. Roll up to form a cylinder and refrigerate until the butter hardens.

Remove the scallops from the marinade, reserving the marinade for basting. Thread four scallops, a strip of orange zest and three chunks of zucchini onto each skewer. Cook the brochettes on a prepared, medium-hot grill for 8-10 minutes, turning and brushing them frequently with the marinade. Serve the hot brochettes with discs of flavored butter, so the butter melts over the scallops and zucchini. SERVES 4

TURMERIC SHRIMP & PINEAPPLE SKEWERS

24 raw jumbo shrimp, peeled but with tails intact
8 wooden or metal skewers
8 ounces fresh pineapple, cut into 16 chunks
16 bulbous white parts of scallion

TURMERIC MARINADE
1 stalk lemon grass, finely chopped
1-inch piece fresh ginger root, peeled and grated
2 cloves garlic, crushed
2 tablespoons peanut oil
1 tablespoon lemon juice
1 teaspoon turmeric
Pinch of sugar
Salt and ground black pepper

Place the marinade ingredients in a food processor and blend to a paste. Transfer the paste to a large bowl, add the shrimp, and turn to coat evenly. Refrigerate for 2-3 hours or overnight.

Thread the marinated shrimp onto the skewers, alternating with the pineapple chunks and scallions. Reserve the marinade for basting. Cook the shrimp skewers on a prepared grill for 8-10 minutes, turning and basting them while they cook. Serve at once.
SERVES 4

LEFT: Turmeric Shrimp & Pineapple Skewers
RIGHT: Scallop Brochettes with
Ginger & Orange

MALAYSIAN FISH WITH SPICY PEANUT SAUCE

6 medium mackerel, weighing about 7 ounces each,
gutted and cleaned
A wire basket for cooking the fish

MARINADE

4 tablespoons sambal oelek (hot chili condiment)
4 tablespoons peanut oil
2 teaspoons brown sugar
2 cloves garlic, crushed
Juice of 2 limes

SPICY PEANUT SAUCE

1 tablespoon tamarind concentrate, mixed with
½ cup water
4 teaspoons brown sugar
2 scallions, chopped
1 stalk lemon grass, chopped
1 clove garlic, crushed
1 tablespoon sambal oelek (hot chili condiment)
¾ cup coarsely ground salted peanuts
⅔ cup coconut milk

Mix the marinade ingredients together in a bowl. Make several deep slashes in the flesh of each mackerel and place the fish in a large, shallow dish. Pour the marinade over and turn the fish around, coating well. Cover and refrigerate for at least 2 hours.

Make the peanut sauce. Place the first six ingredients in a saucepan, bring to a boil, then reduce the heat and simmer for 5 minutes. Add the peanuts and cook for a further minute, then stir in the coconut milk and simmer for a further 3 minutes. Set aside.

Remove the mackerel from the marinade, reserving the marinade for basting. Cook the fish in a wire basket on a prepared grill for about 15 minutes, turning and basting as they cook. Serve the fish with the warm Spicy Peanut Sauce.   SERVES 6

PHUKET CRAB CAKES

2 tablespoons butter
¼ cup all-purpose flour
⅔ cup milk
4 cups fresh or canned crabmeat
2 cups fresh white breadcrumbs
4 tablespoons chopped fresh cilantro
2 tablespoons grated lime zest
3 tablespoons freshly squeezed lime juice
3 tablespoons grated fresh ginger root
4 teaspoons soy sauce
1 fresh red chili, seeded and finely chopped
Salt and ground black pepper
4 tablespoons vegetable oil for brushing
A metal griddle plate for cooking
Salad and hot chili sauce, to serve (optional)

Melt the butter in a saucepan and stir in the flour to make a roux. Gradually add the milk, whisking well between each addition, and boil for 2-3 minutes to make a thick white sauce.

Remove the sauce from the heat and stir in the crabmeat, breadcrumbs, cilantro, lime zest and juice, ginger, soy sauce, chili and seasoning. Let cool.

When the mixture is cool, shape it into eight cakes. Refrigerate the crab cakes for at least 2 hours before cooking them.

Oil the griddle and heat it on a prepared grill. Brush the crab cakes with some oil and cook on the griddle for 4-5 minutes. Brush with more oil, turn the crab cakes over, and cook for a further 4-5 minutes. Serve at once with a salad and chili sauce, if desired.

SERVES 4

RIGHT: Malaysian Fish with Spicy Peanut Sauce

PORK BROCHETTES WITH CITRUS SALSA

1 pound pork tenderloin, cut into 1½-inch cubes
8 wooden or metal skewers
2 yellow bell peppers, cored, seeded and chopped
8 small onions, halved
16 bay leaves

MARINADE

4 tablespoons dry sherry or rice wine
4 tablespoons ground coriander
4 tablespoons sunflower oil
4 cloves garlic, finely chopped
6 lime leaves, finely chopped
Salt and ground black pepper

CITRUS SALSA

2 oranges
2 pink grapefruit
2 teaspoons chopped fresh thyme
4 teaspoons snipped fresh chives
4 lime leaves, very finely chopped
Salt and ground black pepper

Mix the marinade ingredients together in a glass bowl. Add the cubed pork and mix to coat evenly. Cover and refrigerate for 4 hours.

Thread the marinated pork onto the skewers, alternating with the bell peppers, onions and bay leaves. Reserve the marinade for basting.

For the salsa, peel the oranges and grapefruit, and cut in between the membranes to produce sections. Chop the sections roughly. Place in a bowl with the remaining ingredients and toss gently to combine.

Cook the brochettes over a prepared medium-hot grill for about 15 minutes, turning frequently and brushing them with the marinade. Serve hot, accompanied by the Citrus Salsa.   SERVES 4

THAI-STYLE SKEWERED CHICKEN

4 skinless, boneless chicken breasts, weighing
5 ounces each
8 wooden or metal skewers
Lime wedges, to serve
Jasmine and Sesame Rice, to serve (see page 72)

THAI MARINADE

2 tablespoons Thai red curry paste
2 tablespoons ground coriander
3 tablespoons peanut oil
2 teaspoons ground cumin
2 teaspoons superfine sugar
2 stalks lemon grass, very finely chopped
Juice of 2 limes

Mix the marinade ingredients together in a large bowl. Cut the chicken into 1-inch cubes and add to the marinade. Turn to coat evenly, cover, and refrigerate for 2-3 hours or overnight.

Thread the marinated chicken onto the skewers and reserve the remaining marinade for basting. Cook the chicken on a prepared, medium-hot grill for about 7 minutes on each side, basting with the reserved marinade while cooking. Serve with lime wedges and Jasmine and Sesame Rice, if desired.   SERVES 4

TOP: Thai-style Skewered Chicken
BOTTOM: Pork Brochettes with Citrus Salsa

CHARGRILLED SQUID WITH SESAME & CASHEW

2 tablespoons cornstarch, sifted
2 beaten egg whites
2 teaspoons light soy sauce
1 teaspoon sesame oil
1½ cups finely chopped raw cashews
4 tablespoons sesame seeds
12 prepared baby squid tubes
Small wooden skewers
A metal griddle plate for cooking
Thai sweet chili sauce, to serve
Julienne of scallion and cucumber, to serve

STUFFING

4 cups cooked white rice
4 scallions, finely chopped
2 teaspoons finely chopped fresh ginger root
1 teaspoon finely chopped fresh red chili
2 teaspoons light soy sauce

Place the stuffing ingredients in a food processor and blend briefly until well combined. Stuff the cavities of the squid with the mixture.

Mix the cornstarch, egg whites, soy sauce and sesame oil together. Mix the cashews and sesame seeds together, and spread them out on a plate. Dip each stuffed squid tube in the egg mixture and then roll in the cashew mixture to coat evenly. Secure the end of each squid tube with a wooden skewer to hold in the stuffing. Chill the coated squid tubes in the refrigerator for 2 hours.

Oil the griddle plate and heat it on a prepared grill. Cook the squid on the griddle for about 8 minutes, turning occasionally until golden. Serve hot with the chili sauce and vegetable julienne.   SERVES 4

CHINESE-STYLE SPARE RIBS

3 pounds meaty pork spare ribs

SZECHUAN MARINADE

4 stalks lemon grass, very finely chopped
4 tablespoons crushed Szechuan peppercorns
4 tablespoons dried chili flakes
4 tablespoons peanut oil
3 tablespoons brown sugar
4 teaspoons ground coriander
4 teaspoons sesame oil

Place the marinade ingredients in a food processor or spice grinder and blend to a paste. Transfer the marinade to a large bowl.

Cut the spare ribs into 4-inch lengths and add to the bowl of marinade. Turn to coat evenly, cover, and refrigerate for 2-3 hours or overnight.

Remove the ribs from the marinade, reserving the marinade for basting. Cook the ribs on a prepared grill for 15-20 minutes, turning and basting them occasionally. Serve at once.   SERVES 4-6

RIGHT: Chargrilled Squid with Sesame & Cashew

LAMB & APRICOT SKEWERS

1¼ pounds boneless, lean lamb, cut into 24 pieces
4 shallots
4 firm, ripe apricots, halved
16 bay leaves
8 wooden or metal skewers
Barbecued Artichokes, to serve (optional)

MARINADE

3 tablespoons apricot preserves
2 tablespoons soy sauce
4 tablespoons vegetable oil
2 tablespoons cider vinegar
¾ teaspoon cayenne pepper
2 large cloves garlic, crushed
Ground black pepper

Mix the marinade ingredients together in a shallow glass dish. Add the lamb pieces, toss to coat evenly, cover, and refrigerate for 2 hours.

Blanch the shallots in boiling water for 4 minutes, then remove, peel, and halve them.

Remove the lamb from the marinade, reserving the marinade for basting. Thread three chunks of meat, a shallot half, an apricot half and two bay leaves onto each skewer. Cook the lamb skewers on a prepared grill for about 15 minutes, turning and basting them while cooking. Serve hot with Barbecued Artichokes, if desired.
SERVES 4

BARBECUED ARTICHOKES

4 small globe artichokes
4 tablespoons olive oil
Juice of ½ lemon
Salt and ground black pepper

Trim the artichoke stalks close to the base and cook them in boiling, salted water for 20-25 minutes.

Halve the artichokes and scoop out the prickly chokes. Mix together the oil, lemon juice and seasoning. Brush the artichokes all over with the oil mixture and cook on a prepared grill for 10-15 minutes, turning occasionally, until they are lightly charred. Serve hot.
SERVES 4

SPICY BEEF KABOBS

1¼ pounds fillet or rump steak, cut into
bite-size cubes
1 red bell pepper
1 green bell pepper
1 yellow bell pepper
16 cherry tomatoes
8 metal skewers

GINGER MARINADE

2 tablespoons vegetable oil
4 tablespoons red wine
½ cup balsamic vinegar
3 tablespoons grated fresh ginger root
2 teaspoons paprika
2 teaspoons cayenne pepper
Salt and ground black pepper

Mix the marinade ingredients together in a shallow glass dish. Add the cubed beef and toss to coat evenly. Cover and refrigerate for 2-3 hours or overnight.

Halve the bell peppers and remove the cores and seeds. Cut the peppers into 1-inch cubes.

Remove the beef from the marinade, reserving the marinade for basting. Thread the beef, peppers and cherry tomatoes onto the skewers. Cook the kabobs on a prepared grill for 10-12 minutes, turning and basting them while they are cooking.
SERVES 4

TOP: Barbecued Artichokes
BOTTOM: Lamb & Apricot Skewers,
Spicy Beef Kabobs

AROMATIC BARBECUES

The blends of herbs and spices used in the recipes in this chapter evoke the warmth of the Mediterranean. Chicken Bagna Cauda combines the classic Southern Italian ingredients of anchovies, sun-dried tomatoes, garlic and olive oil, while the Eastern Mediterranean Kofta Kabobs use mint, garlic, cumin and cilantro to reproduce the aromatic flavors of that region. Sage, thyme, rosemary, saffron, cayenne pepper and peppercorns are used liberally in the recipes to produce enticing aromas, guaranteed to whet most appetites.

SURF & TURF GRILL

1 pound fillet steak, cut into 1-inch cubes
8 medium scallops
8 raw jumbo shrimp, shelled but with tails left intact
4 long metal skewers
Herby rice and salad, to serve (optional)

MARINADE
4 tablespoons corn oil
4 tablespoons Bourbon whiskey
Grated zest and juice of 2 limes
Salt and ground black pepper

Place the marinade ingredients in a shallow glass dish and mix well. Add the steak, scallops and shrimp to the marinade, cover, and refrigerate for 4 hours.

Remove the marinated food from the marinade, reserving the marinade for basting, and thread the steak, scallops and shrimp onto the skewers.

Cook the skewers on a prepared grill for 8-10 minutes, basting them while they are cooking. Serve with herby rice and a salad, if desired.   SERVES 4

BLACKENED SEA BASS

4 sea bass fillets, weighing 5 ounces each
4 tablespoons melted butter
Lemon wedges, to serve
Skewered New Potatoes, to serve (see page 74)

SPICE MIX
1 teaspoon salt
1 teaspoon garlic flakes
1 teaspoon dried parsley
1 teaspoon chili powder
½ teaspoon ground bay leaves
1 tablespoon cayenne pepper
Ground black pepper

BUTTER SAUCE
3 tablespoons dry white wine
2 tablespoons white wine vinegar
¼ cup cubed butter
⅔ cup heavy cream
1 tablespoon chopped fresh parsley
1 tablespoon snipped fresh chives

Mix the spice mix ingredients together and place on a plate. Brush the sea bass fillets all over with melted butter, then place on the spice mix and turn to coat evenly. Cover and refrigerate the fillets for 1 hour.

Cook the fish on the oiled rack of a prepared grill for 3-4 minutes on each side.

Just before serving, make the sauce. Place the wine and vinegar in a saucepan and boil rapidly for 1-2 minutes to reduce it by half. Then whisk in the butter, a cube at a time, over a low heat. Add the cream and cook for 1-2 minutes, whisking. Stir in the herbs and serve with the sea bass, lemon and potatoes.

SERVES 4

RIGHT: Blackened Sea Bass

SEAFOOD BROCHETTES

12 ounces skinless, boneless salmon steak
12 ounces skinless, boneless angler fish
16 raw jumbo shrimp
8 metal skewers

CHERVIL MARINADE

4 tablespoons sunflower oil
½ cup chopped fresh chervil
Salt and ground black pepper

SAFFRON SAUCE

1 tablespoon sunflower oil
2 shallots, finely chopped
2½ cups dry white wine
½ teaspoon saffron threads, soaked in
2 tablespoons boiling water
1¼ cups light cream
2 tablespoons chopped fresh chervil
2 tablespoons snipped fresh chives
Salt and ground black pepper

Cut the salmon and angler fish into 16 chunks each. Place the fish and shrimp in a shallow glass dish. Mix the marinade ingredients together and pour over. Toss to coat evenly, cover, and refrigerate for 2 hours.

Make the Saffron Sauce. Heat the oil in a saucepan and sauté the shallots for 3 minutes. Add the wine and saffron with the water, bring to a boil, and boil steadily for 10-12 minutes, until liquid has reduced to about one-quarter of its original amount. Add the cream and reduce again for 4-5 minutes. Add the herbs and seasoning, and heat for a further 30 seconds. Set aside.

Remove the fish and shrimp from the marinade, reserving the marinade for basting, and divide them equally between the skewers. Cook on the oiled rack of a prepared grill for 8-10 minutes, turning and brushing with marinade. Reheat the sauce and serve it at once with the brochettes.   SERVES 4

CRUMBED OYSTERS WITH PIQUANT TOMATO DIP

16 fresh oysters
4 tablespoons butter
¾ cup fresh white breadcrumbs
2 scallions, finely chopped
1 tablespoon chopped fresh thyme
Generous pinch of paprika
Salt and ground black pepper

PIQUANT TOMATO DIP

1 pound tomatoes, roughly chopped
4 scallions, finely chopped
2 teaspoons grated horseradish
2 teaspoons Worcestershire sauce
1 teaspoon sugar
Few drops Tabasco sauce
Salt and ground black pepper

Prepare the tomato dip. Place the tomatoes in a food processor and blend briefly to produce a thick puree. Transfer the tomatoes to a saucepan, add the remaining ingredients, and bring to a boil. Boil steadily for about 10 minutes to produce a thick sauce. Taste and adjust seasoning, if necessary, and set aside.

Open the oysters, leaving them on the half shell. Melt the butter in a skillet, add the breadcrumbs, and cook for 1 minute. Stir in the remaining ingredients and cook for 3-4 minutes, stirring constantly.

Top each oyster with a little of the crispy breadcrumb mixture, making sure the coating covers the oysters. Cook the oysters on a prepared grill for 4-5 minutes, until the oysters are lightly cooked and heated through. Reheat the tomato dip and serve it with the oysters.   SERVES 4 AS A STARTER

TOP: Crumbed Oysters with Piquant
Tomato Dip
BOTTOM: Seafood Brochettes

CAJUN TURKEY KABOBS

1¼ pounds turkey breast, cut into 1-inch cubes
8 wooden or metal skewers
8 baby corn, blanched for 1 minute
8 shallots, blanched for 5 minutes and peeled
1 large green bell pepper, cored, seeded
and chopped
16 bay leaves
2 tablespoons corn oil
Saffron rice, to serve (optional)

MARINADE
1 small onion, chopped
2 cloves garlic, chopped
1 tablespoon chopped fresh oregano
1 tablespoon chopped fresh thyme
1½ teaspoons paprika
½ teaspoon cayenne pepper
Juice of ½ lemon
4 tablespoons corn oil
Salt and ground black pepper

Place the marinade ingredients in a food processor and blend to a smooth paste. Pour the marinade into a glass bowl and add the cubed turkey, turning to coat well. Cover and refrigerate for 4 hours.

Thread the marinated turkey onto the skewers, alternating with the baby corn, shallots, bell peppers and bay leaves.

Add the corn oil to the remaining marinade in the dish and brush over the kabobs while cooking them.

Cook the kabobs on a prepared, medium-hot grill for about 7 minutes on each side, brushing them with the reserved marinade. Serve at once with the saffron rice, if desired.   SERVES 4

CREOLE-STYLE PORK SKEWERS

1¼ pounds pork tenderloin, cut into 24 pieces
8 wooden or metal skewers
1 large red onion, cut into 8 wedges
1 large yellow bell pepper, cored, seeded and cut into chunks

MARINADE
4 tablespoons olive oil
2 tablespoons sun-dried tomato paste
2 tablespoons tomato ketchup
2 tablespoons lemon juice
2 cloves garlic, crushed
2 small pickled green chilies, chopped
Salt and ground black pepper

Mix all the marinade ingredients together. Pour the marinade into a shallow glass dish and add the pork pieces, turning to coat well. Cover and refrigerate for 4 hours.

Remove the pork from the marinade, reserving the marinade for basting, and thread the pork onto the skewers with the onions and bell peppers.

Cook the pork skewers on a prepared, medium-hot grill for 12-15 minutes, basting them with the reserved marinade while they are cooking.   SERVES 4

RIGHT: Cajun Turkey Kabobs

CHICKEN PINWHEELS

4 skinless, boneless chicken breasts, weighing
5 ounces each
4-ounce piece leek, cut into 2 lengths
3 tablespoons olive oil for brushing
Rice, to serve (optional)

STUFFING

¼ cup finely chopped pistachio nuts
⅓ cup fresh white breadcrumbs
4 tablespoons melted butter
24 basil leaves, torn
Salt and ground black pepper

BASIL CREAM SAUCE

1¼ cups light cream
16 large basil leaves, torn
Ground black pepper

Place the stuffing ingredients in a bowl and mix well.

Place a chicken breast between two pieces of waxed paper and pound with a meat pounder to flatten. Repeat with the remaining chicken breasts.

Blanch the leeks for 3 minutes, then drain and refresh in cold water. Slice each piece of leek in half lengthwise. Dry the pieces of leek on paper towels.

Spread one-quarter of the stuffing onto each chicken breast, leaving a ½-inch border around the edges. Place a piece of leek in the center, then roll up to enclose the stuffing. Secure with string. Repeat with the remaining chicken. Refrigerate for 2 hours.

Brush the pinwheels with a little olive oil and cook on a prepared grill for 20-25 minutes, turning and brushing them with more oil as they cook.

Make the sauce. Place the cream, basil and seasoning in a saucepan, and bring to a boil. Boil rapidly for 4-5 minutes, until the sauce has reduced slightly. To serve, slice the chicken pinwheels thickly and serve with some sauce and rice.   SERVES 4

CHICKEN BAGNA CAUDA

4 boneless chicken breasts with skin, weighing about
6 ounces each
4 tablespoons chopped fresh parsley
4 tablespoons olive oil
4 cloves garlic, crushed
Salt and ground black pepper
Polenta or pasta, to serve (optional)

ANCHOVY SAUCE

1 cup olive oil
4 cloves garlic, crushed
8 anchovy fillets, finely chopped
12 halves sun-dried tomatoes in oil, drained and finely chopped
2 tablespoons chili sauce
2 tablespoons chopped fresh parsley
Ground black pepper

Make several deep slashes through the skin and flesh of each chicken breast. Mix the chopped parsley, oil, garlic and seasoning together. Work this mixture into the slashes and over the surface of each chicken breast. Place the chicken in a shallow dish, pour over any remaining mixture, cover, and refrigerate for 2 hours.

Make the sauce. Heat the oil in a saucepan and sauté the garlic for 1 minute. Add the remaining ingredients and simmer gently for 3-4 minutes. Set the sauce aside until required.

Remove the chicken from the dish, reserving any remaining mixture for basting. Cook the chicken breasts on a prepared grill for about 20 minutes, turning and basting occasionally. Test the chicken with a skewer: if juices run clear, the chicken is cooked.

Reheat the sauce and serve it with the cooked chicken and the cooked polenta or pasta.   SERVES 4

TOP: Chicken Pinwheels
BOTTOM: Chicken Bagna Cauda

AROMATIC DUCK BREASTS WITH PORT & CHERRIES

4 duck breasts, weighing 7 ounces each
New potatoes, to serve (optional)

MARINADE
4 tablespoons chopped fresh rosemary
4 teaspoons ground cinnamon
2 teaspoons ground allspice
I teaspoon brown sugar
3 tablespoons vegetable oil

PORT AND CHERRY SAUCE
1½ cups ruby port
½ cup red wine vinegar
4 teaspoons brown sugar
I cup fresh cherries, halved, or
⅔ cup pitted whole canned cherries
Salt and ground black pepper

Make several deep slashes through the skin and flesh of each duck breast. Mix the marinade ingredients together and work this mixture into the slashes and surface of the duck breasts. Cover and refrigerate for at least 2 hours.

Make the sauce. Place the port, vinegar and sugar in a saucepan, and bring to a boil. Boil the sauce for 4-5 minutes to reduce it, then add the cherries. Reduce the heat and cook very gently for a further 6-8 minutes. Taste and adjust seasoning, if necessary, and set the sauce aside until required.

Cook the duck breasts on a prepared, medium-hot grill for about 10 minutes on each side, until cooked through. Reheat the sauce. Slice the duck breasts and serve them with the Port and Cherry Sauce and potatoes, if desired. SERVES 4

BBQ DUCK WITH SAGE & ORANGE STUFFING

4 leg portions of duck

SAGE AND ORANGE STUFFING
4 tablespoons softened butter
2 teaspoons dry mustard powder
4 tablespoons very finely chopped celery
8 sage leaves, chopped
Grated zest of I large orange
Salt and ground black pepper

MARINADE
Juice of I large orange
2 sage leaves, chopped
4 tablespoons orange marmalade
I tablespoon vegetable oil

Mix the ingredients for the stuffing together in a bowl. Loosen the skin of the duck portions by easing it away from the leg meat. Divide the stuffing between the duck portions, placing it between the skin and leg meat, and spreading it out as much as possible.

Mix together the marinade ingredients. Place the duck portions in a shallow glass dish, pour over the marinade, then cover and refrigerate for at least 2 hours or overnight.

Remove the duck from the marinade, reserving the marinade for basting. Cook the duck on a prepared grill for 20-25 minutes, turning and basting the duck while it is cooking. Serve at once. SERVES 4

TOP: Aromatic Duck Breasts with Port & Cherries
BOTTOM: BBQ Duck with Sage & Orange Stuffing

KOFTA KABOBS

12 ounces ground lamb

4 slices crustless white bread, crumbled

1 onion, finely chopped

4 cloves garlic, crushed

4 tablespoons chopped fresh mint

2 tablespoons chopped fresh parsley

4 tablespoons toasted pine nuts

2 tablespoons raisins

2 tablespoons lightly toasted cumin seeds

1 teaspoon ground coriander

1 beaten egg

Salt and ground black pepper

4 metal skewers

Oil for brushing

1½ cups shredded iceberg lettuce

2 tomatoes, cut into wedges

1 onion, sliced

12 black olives

Warm pita bread and lemon wedges, to serve

MINT DRESSING

⅔ cup Greek yogurt

4 tablespoons chopped fresh mint

Pinch of cayenne pepper

Salt and ground black pepper

Place the first 12 ingredients in a food processor and process briefly to combine. Divide the mixture into 12 portions and shape each portion into an oval-shaped patty. Refrigerate for 2 hours.

Mix the Mint Dressing ingredients together in a bowl and refrigerate until required.

Thread three koftas onto each skewer and brush with a little oil. Cook on a prepared grill for 6 minutes on each side, turning and brushing with oil.

Divide the lettuce, tomato, onion and olives between four plates. Add the kabobs, and serve at once with the dressing, pita and lemon.   SERVES 4

PEPPERED STEAKS WITH HERB COUSCOUS

4 beef fillet steaks, weighing 5 ounces each

4 teaspoons olive oil

4 tablespoons crushed mixed peppercorns

HERB COUSCOUS

1 cup couscous

2 cups boiling water

2 tablespoons olive oil

4 scallions, finely chopped

½ cup chopped fresh parsley

Finely grated zest of 1 large lemon

4 teaspoons lemon juice

1 red bell pepper, broiled, skinned and diced

Salt and ground black pepper

Brush each steak with a little olive oil and press the crushed peppercorns onto the surfaces.

Place the couscous in a bowl with a little salt and pour the boiling water over the top. Let the couscous stand for 5-10 minutes, until the water has been absorbed and the grains have swelled up.

Cook the peppered steaks on the oiled rack of a prepared grill for about 5 minutes on each side, turning them halfway through cooking.

Just before serving, finish the couscous by heating the oil in a large saucepan, adding the couscous and all the remaining ingredients, and stirring to combine and heat through. Serve the peppered steaks with the couscous.   SERVES 4

RIGHT: Kofta Kabobs

BBQ VEAL ROLLS

4 veal scallops, weighing 5 ounces each
2 ounces fresh spinach
I tablespoon olive oil
2 large cloves garlic, chopped
2 tablespoons finely chopped red onion
½ cup ricotta cheese
4 teaspoons toasted pine nuts
Salt and ground black pepper
Barbecued Artichokes, to serve (see page 36)

MARINADE

6 tablespoons white wine
3 tablespoons olive oil
Pinch of nutmeg
Ground black pepper

Place a veal scallop between two pieces of waxed paper and pound with a meat pounder or mallet to flatten. Repeat with the remaining veal scallops.

Steam the spinach, then lay the leaves on paper towels to remove any excess moisture. Heat the oil in a saucepan, add the garlic and onion, and sauté for 1-2 minutes until soft. Transfer to a large bowl and stir in the ricotta cheese, pine nuts and seasoning.

Season a veal scallop, then place one-quarter of the spinach in a layer over the veal, leaving a ½-inch border around the edges. Season again and spread one-quarter of the ricotta mixture over the spinach. Roll the veal scallop up to completely enclose the filling. Secure with string. Repeat with the remaining veal, spinach and ricotta mixture.

Place the marinade ingredients in a shallow glass dish and mix well. Add the veal rolls to the dish and turn to coat evenly. Cover and refrigerate for 2 hours.

Remove the veal rolls from the marinade, reserving the marinade for basting. Cook on a prepared grill for about 20 minutes, turning and basting. Serve at once with Barbecued Artichokes.   SERVES 4

PECAN-COATED TURKEY SCALLOPS

4 turkey scallops, weighing 4 ounces each
2 tablespoons Dijon mustard
2 tablespoons sour cream
I cup coarsely ground pecans
Oil for brushing
Lemon wedges, to serve

SOUR CREAM DIP

6 tablespoons sour cream
2 tablespoons snipped fresh chives
2 teaspoons Dijon mustard
Lemon juice to taste
Salt and ground black pepper

Place the turkey scallops between two pieces of waxed paper and pound them with a meat pounder or mallet to flatten.

Mix together the Dijon mustard and sour cream, and place the ground pecans on a flat plate. Dip a scallop in the mustard mixture, and then place it on the plate of pecans and turn to coat evenly. Repeat with the remaining turkey. Cover and refrigerate for at least 2 hours before barbecuing.

Mix the ingredients for the dip together, cover, and refrigerate until required.

Brush the pecan-coated turkey scallops with a little oil and cook them on a prepared grill for 6-7 minutes on each side, until they are golden and cooked through. Serve hot with lemon wedges and the Sour Cream Dip.   SERVES 4

TOP: Pecan-coated Turkey Scallops
BOTTOM: BBQ Veal Rolls

VEGETABLE BARBECUES

Recipes for first courses, side dishes and main courses are included in this chapter, enabling you to create a totally vegetarian meal, if desired. Although some recipes would not immediately be associated with barbecues, they work very well. For example, the Savoy Cabbage Parcels and the Grape Leaves with Feta, Olives & Tomato are novel barbecue ideas, but delicious. Some recipes will require a little extra care with handling, as the ingredients are more fragile than traditional barbecue ingredients.

SPICED CORN ON THE COB

4 corn on the cob, husks removed
2 tablespoons olive oil
½ teaspoon cayenne pepper
Salt and ground black pepper

CHILI BUTTER

6 tablespoons softened butter
2 tablespoons coarsely chopped fresh cilantro
2 teaspoons finely chopped fresh red chili
Salt and ground black pepper

Prepare the Chili Butter. Mix the ingredients together until thoroughly combined. Place the butter in an oblong shape on a piece of plastic wrap or parchment paper. Roll up to form a cylinder and refrigerate to harden the butter.

Cook the corn in plenty of boiling, salted water for about 15 minutes, until it is tender. Drain, then toss the corn in the olive oil, cayenne pepper and seasoning to coat well.

Cook the corn on a prepared grill for 10-15 minutes, turning occasionally while cooking. They are ready to serve when they are slightly charred. Serve at once with discs of Chili Butter. SERVES 4

MEDITERRANEAN VEGETABLES

The quantity of herb oil in this recipe is sufficient to cook the vegetables listed below. Vegetables may be varied according to preference.

4 corn on the cob
8 baby Florence fennel bulbs
4 plum tomatoes
2 red onions
2 bell peppers, any color

HERB AND GARLIC OIL

⅔ cup extra virgin olive oil
2 tablespoons balsamic vinegar
2 cloves garlic, crushed
½ cup chopped fresh mixed herbs, such as Florence fennel fronds, chives, parsley and basil
Salt and ground black pepper

Prepare the vegetables for barbecuing. Peel back the husks from the corn and knot them at the base. Remove all the silks from the corn and discard. Trim the baby Florence fennel and halve the tomatoes. Halve the onions, leaving the skins intact. Halve the bell peppers lengthwise and remove the cores and seeds, leaving the stalks intact.

Mix the ingredients for the Herb and Garlic Oil together. To cook the vegetables, brush them liberally with the herb oil and cook on a prepared grill, turning and brushing frequently until they are cooked through and slightly charred. The corn on the cob will take about 20 minutes to cook, the onions 15-20 minutes, and the fennel, tomatoes and peppers about 10 minutes to cook. SERVES 4-6

RIGHT: Mediterranean Vegetables

HALLOUMI, ZUCCHINI & MUSHROOM SKEWERS

These cheese and vegetable skewers make a satisfying vegetarian main course when served with a tomato and olive salad and warm pita bread.

12 ounces halloumi cheese
1 red bell pepper, halved, cored and seeded
6 ounces zucchini, cut into 8 chunks
8 large mushrooms, halved
½ cup extra virgin olive oil
2 tablespoons chopped fresh thyme
2 cloves garlic, chopped
Ground black pepper
8 wooden or metal skewers

Cut the cheese and red bell pepper into 1-inch squares. Place them in a shallow dish with the zucchini and mushrooms. Mix the olive oil, thyme, garlic and pepper together, and pour over the vegetables. Toss gently to coat evenly, then thread the cheese and vegetables onto the skewers. Brush with any remaining oil mixture.

Cook on the oiled rack of a prepared grill for about 8 minutes, turning occasionally and brushing with any remaining oil mixture. The skewers are ready to serve when the halloumi cheese is golden and the vegetables are tender. SERVES 4

SPICY POTATO, SHALLOT & FENNEL KABOBS

Baby Florence fennel bulbs are used in this recipe, but, if they are unavailable, substitute small wedges of ordinary Florence fennel.

24 baby new potatoes
8 small shallots
16 baby Florence fennel bulbs, about 10 ounces in total weight
4 teaspoons mustard seeds
4 teaspoons cumin seeds
4 teaspoons garam masala
2 teaspoons turmeric
4 teaspoons lemon juice
½ cup peanut oil
Salt and ground black pepper
8 wooden or metal skewers

Cook the potatoes in boiling, salted water for about 12 minutes until tender. Drain and transfer to a large mixing bowl. Cook the shallots in boiling water for 4 minutes, drain, and, when cool enough to handle, peel them. Add to the potatoes, along with the fennel.

Crush the mustard and cumin seeds lightly and place them in a bowl with the garam masala, turmeric, lemon juice, peanut oil and some seasoning. Mix to combine, then pour over the prepared vegetables and toss to coat well. Cover and refrigerate for 2 hours, if time permits.

Remove the vegetables from the mixture, reserving any remaining mixture for brushing, and thread the vegetables evenly between the skewers. Cook the kabobs on a prepared grill for about 12 minutes, turning and brushing while cooking. SERVES 4

TOP: Spicy Potato, Shallot & Fennel Kabobs
BOTTOM: Halloumi, Zucchini & Mushroom Skewers

GRILLED VEGETABLES WITH TAHINI DRESSING

12 ounces sweet potato, peeled and cut into 4 slices
1 pound celeriac, peeled and cut into 4 slices
12 ounces pumpkin, peeled and cut into 4 wedges
2 medium parsnips, peeled and halved lengthwise
6 tablespoons olive oil for brushing
Sea salt and ground black pepper

TAHINI DRESSING

4 tablespoons light tahini
4 tablespoons mayonnaise
3 tablespoons olive oil
¼ teaspoon paprika
2 cloves garlic, crushed
2 scallions, chopped
2 teaspoons lemon juice
Salt and ground black pepper

Mix the ingredients for the dressing together in a bowl and refrigerate until required.

Cook the different types of root vegetables individually in boiling, salted water, until they are just tender. The celeriac will take about 12 minutes to cook, the sweet potato 10 minutes, the parsnip 8 minutes, and the pumpkin 6 minutes.

Drain the cooked vegetables and dry them on paper towels. Brush them all over with olive oil and season generously with salt and pepper.

Cook the vegetables on the oiled rack of a prepared grill for about 6 minutes on each side, turning them halfway through cooking and brushing occasionally with oil. Serve the barbecued vegetables with the Tahini Dressing.   SERVES 4

CHARGRILLED YAMS & PLANTAINS WITH HOT PEPPER MAYONNAISE

Green, unripe plantains can be substituted for the half-ripe plantains in this recipe, but they will take longer to cook.

4 × 5-ounce slices yam, peeled
4 × 3-ounce thick slices half-ripe plantain, with skins left intact
Corn oil for brushing
Salt and ground black pepper

HOT PEPPER MAYONNAISE

6 tablespoons mayonnaise
2 tablespoons chopped fresh thyme
1 teaspoon finely chopped habanero chili
4 teaspoons freshly squeezed lime juice
Salt and ground black pepper

Cook the yam slices in boiling, salted water for 15 minutes, or until tender. Drain and set aside until required. Mix the mayonnaise ingredients together and refrigerate until required.

Brush the yam and plantain slices all over with corn oil, and season with salt and pepper. Cook on a prepared grill, turning occasionally until they are tender and charred on the outside. The yams will be ready to serve in 15 minutes and the plantains in about 12 minutes. Serve at once with the mayonnaise.

SERVES 4 AS A STARTER

TOP: Chargrilled Yams & Plantains with Hot Pepper Mayonnaise
BOTTOM: Grilled Vegetables with Tahini Dressing

SAVOY CABBAGE PARCELS

These wrapped cabbage parcels make an excellent accompaniment to barbecued pork or chicken.

4 large Savoy or pointed green cabbage leaves
6 tablespoons butter
1 cup thinly sliced leeks
1 cup coarsely grated carrots
2¼ cups cooked brown rice
¼ cup lightly toasted pumpkin seeds
2 tablespoons chopped fresh tarragon
Salt and ground black pepper

Cut away the tough stalks from the cabbage leaves, then blanch the leaves in boiling, salted water for 1-2 minutes until they are just tender. Drain and refresh in cold water, then place cabbage leaves on paper towels to dry them.

Melt 4 tablespoons of the butter in a saucepan, add the leeks, and sauté for 3 minutes. Stir in the carrot and sauté for a further minute. Remove the pan from the heat and stir in the rice, pumpkin seeds, tarragon and seasoning.

Lay a cabbage leaf on a large piece of foil and place one-quarter of the rice mixture in the center. Fold the cabbage around the filling to form a parcel, dot with one-quarter of the remaining butter, and fold up the foil to enclose the cabbage. Repeat with the remaining cabbage leaves and filling.

Cook the foil parcels on a prepared grill for 13-15 minutes, until the cabbage is tender and the filling heated through.   SERVES 4

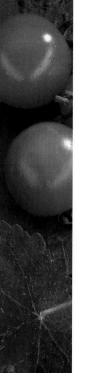

GRAPE LEAVES WITH FETA, OLIVES & TOMATO

8 large vacuum-packed grape leaves
2 tablespoons olive oil
1 cup cubed feta cheese
16 small black olives
8 cherry tomatoes, halved
8 sprigs fresh oregano
Ground black pepper
Small wooden skewers
Greek-style sesame bread, to serve (optional)

Rinse the grape leaves and dry them on paper towels. Place them on a flat surface and brush each leaf with a little olive oil.

Divide the feta, black olives, tomatoes and oregano evenly between the leaves, placing them in the center of each leaf. Grind over some black pepper and fold the leaves around the filling to enclose it completely. Secure the grape leaf bundles with skewers.

Brush the outside of the bundles with the remaining oil and cook them on a prepared grill for about 4-5 minutes, until the cheese has begun to melt. They do not need to be turned, but do keep the skewered side of the bundles upright, away from the coals.

Serve two grape leaves to each person. Peel away the leaves and eat the filling. The leaves are purely to enclose the filling and are not meant to be eaten. Serve with sesame bread, if desired.

SERVES 4 AS A STARTER

RIGHT: Grape Leaves with Feta, Olives & Tomato

PATTYPAN, ONION & EGGPLANT KABOBS

16 small pattypan squash
8 baby eggplants, halved lengthwise
8 baby onions, unpeeled
8 wooden or metal skewers

MARINADE
4 tablespoons chopped fresh cilantro
½ cup olive oil
1 teaspoon garam masala
1 teaspoon dried chili flakes
2 cloves garlic, crushed
Salt and ground black pepper

BULGHUR WHEAT PILAF
1⅓ cups bulghur wheat
3 cups boiling vegetable stock
4 tablespoons olive oil
1 onion, chopped
2 cloves garlic, crushed
1 teaspoon ground cumin
¼ cup raisins
4 tablespoons coarsely chopped cilantro
Salt and ground black pepper

Mix the marinade ingredients together in a large bowl. Boil the pattypan squash for 4 minutes, drain, and add to the marinade, along with the eggplant. Boil the onions for 5 minutes, then drain, peel and halve them. Add the onions to the bowl of vegetables. Toss gently to coat evenly. Cover and refrigerate for 2 hours.

Make the pilaf. Soak the bulghur wheat in the boiling stock for about 40 minutes, until the grains have swelled and are tender. Drain well. Heat the oil in a saucepan, and sauté the onion, garlic and cumin for 4 minutes until soft. Remove from the heat and stir in the bulghur wheat, raisins and cilantro. Season the pilaf generously and set aside until required.

Thread the marinated vegetables evenly between the skewers, reserving the marinade for brushing. Cook the kabobs on a prepared grill for about 10 minutes, turning and brushing occasionally while cooking. Serve at once with the pilaf. SERVES 4

ORIENTAL TOFU SKEWERS

9 ounces tofu, cut into 16 cubes
1 large orange bell pepper, broiled, skinned and cut into 8 long strips
8 cherry tomatoes
3 ounces broccoli, divided into 8 florets
8 wooden or metal skewers
Noodles, to serve (optional)

SESAME MARINADE
3 tablespoons vegetable oil
1 tablespoon sesame oil
1 tablespoon soy sauce
1 teaspoon grated fresh ginger root
1 teaspoon sesame seeds
2 tablespoons rice wine vinegar
1 scallion, finely chopped

Mix the marinade ingredients together in a large bowl. Add the tofu cubes to the marinade, toss gently to coat, cover, and refrigerate for 2 hours.

Remove the tofu from the marinade, reserving the remaining marinade for brushing. Thread the tofu, bell pepper strips, tomatoes and broccoli on the skewers.

Cook the skewers on a prepared grill for 8-10 minutes, turning and brushing them while cooking. Just before serving, pour any remaining marinade over the tofu skewers. Serve with noodles, if desired.
SERVES 4

TOP AND BOTTOM: Oriental Tofu Skewers
CENTER: Pattypan, Onion & Eggplant Kabobs

FALAFEL PATTIES WITH YOGURT & MINT DIP

2 tablespoons vegetable oil
I teaspoon cumin seeds
I onion, finely chopped
2 cloves garlic, crushed
I teaspoon chopped fresh green chili
½ teaspoon turmeric
2 cups canned chickpeas
Salt and ground black pepper
⅔ cup fresh white breadcrumbs
I beaten egg
2 tablespoons chopped fresh cilantro
Flour for coating
Oil for brushing
A flat metal griddle plate or wire basket for cooking
Lemon wedges and pita bread, to serve

YOGURT AND MINT DIP
½ cup Greek yogurt
4 tablespoons chopped fresh mint
I teaspoon lemon juice
Pinch of ground cumin
Salt and ground black pepper

Mix the ingredients for the dip together, cover, and refrigerate until required.

Heat the vegetable oil in a skillet, add cumin seeds, onion and garlic, and sauté for 5 minutes. Add chili and turmeric, and cook for a further 2 minutes. Transfer the spice mixture to a food processor, add the chickpeas and seasoning, and blend briefly until the chickpeas are roughly mashed and thoroughly combined with the spices.

Transfer to a bowl and add the breadcrumbs, egg and cilantro. Mix to combine and divide into eight portions. With floured hands, shape into patties and refrigerate the falafel for about 4 hours.

Oil the griddle plate and heat on a prepared grill or, alternatively, place the falafel in a wire basket. Brush the falafel all over with oil and cook on the grill for 6-7 minutes on each side. Serve hot with the dip, lemon and pita. SERVES 4

PEPPERS STUFFED WITH NUTTY RICE

4 medium red bell peppers
Oil for brushing

NUTTY RICE
I cup basmati rice
I teaspoon saffron threads, infused in
2 tablespoons boiling water for 10 minutes
4 tablespoons vegetable oil
I red onion, thinly sliced
4 small cloves garlic, crushed
½ cup toasted pine nuts
¼ cup coarsely chopped pistachio nuts
4 tablespoons chopped fresh parsley
Salt and ground black pepper

Prepare the Nutty Rice. Cook the basmati rice in boiling, salted water, to which the saffron and its water has been added. The rice will take 8-10 minutes to cook. Drain and place the rice in a mixing bowl.

Heat the oil in a pan and sauté the onion and garlic for 2-3 minutes. Add to the rice, with the pine nuts, pistachios, parsley and seasoning. Toss to combine.

Halve the bell peppers lengthwise and core and seed, leaving the stalks intact. Divide the Nutty Rice between the pepper halves. Lightly oil four large pieces of foil and place two pepper halves on each piece of foil. Fold up each foil package and cook on a prepared grill for about 20 minutes, until the peppers are tender and the rice is hot. SERVES 4

RIGHT: Falafel Patties with Yogurt & Mint Dip

MUSHROOM & MOZZARELLA BROCHETTES

Rosemary branches can be used in this recipe to skewer the food. Choose long, mature branches and strip off the leaves, leaving just a few at the top. Soak them in cold water for 1 hour.

16 fresh shiitake mushrooms, about 4 ounces in total weight
16 button mushrooms, about 8 ounces in total weight
16 mini mozzarella cheese balls
8 metal or rosemary branch skewers
Steamed couscous, to serve (optional)

MARINADE
Zest and juice of 2 small lemons
2 tablespoons olive oil
3 tablespoons chopped fresh rosemary
2 teaspoons chili oil
½ small fresh red chili, seeded and finely chopped
½ small fresh green chili, seeded and finely chopped
2 cloves garlic, crushed
Salt and ground black pepper

Mix the marinade ingredients together. Place the two types of mushrooms and the mini mozzarellas in a mixing bowl. Pour the marinade over and toss gently to coat evenly. Cover and refrigerate for 2 hours.

Remove the marinated mushrooms and cheese from the dish, reserving any remaining marinade for brushing, and thread the mushrooms and cheese evenly between the skewers or rosemary branches.

Cook the brochettes on a prepared medium-hot grill for about 10 minutes, turning and brushing them while cooking. Serve at once with steamed couscous, if desired. SERVES 4

GOAT CHEESE, LEEK & WALNUT BRUSCHETTA

6 slices French bread, cut on an acute angle
3 tablespoons olive oil
6 × 1½-ounce slices soft goat cheese
Ground black pepper

LEEK AND WALNUT TOPPING
2 tablespoons olive oil
¾ cup thinly sliced leeks
2 tablespoons coarsely chopped walnuts
Salt and ground black pepper

Make the topping. Heat the oil in a saucepan and sauté the leeks for about 3 minutes, until they are soft. Remove from the heat and stir in the remaining ingredients. Set aside until required.

Brush both sides of the sliced bread with 2 tablespoons of the olive oil. Place the bread on the rack of a prepared grill and cook for 2-3 minutes, until toasted on one side. Do not toast the other side.

Remove from the grill and divide the Leek and Walnut Topping between the toasted sides of the bread slices. Top each slice with a piece of goat cheese and drizzle with the remaining olive oil. Grind over some black pepper.

Return the bruschetta to the grill and cook for a further 3-4 minutes, until the cheese begins to melt. Serve at once. SERVES 6 AS A STARTER

LEFT AND BOTTOM: Goat Cheese, Leek & Walnut Bruschetta
RIGHT: Mushroom & Mozzarella Brochettes

SWEET DESSERTS

The recipes in this chapter allow you to extend your barbecue meal to the last course (provided that the coals have been tended so they are still glowing). Fruits lend themselves to barbecuing, as they cook quickly and combine well with other flavors. Barbecued bananas are a classic favorite and here made more special by adding a maple syrup and pecan sauce. Tamarillos with Brown Sugar are extremely easy to prepare, yet produce a delicious and unusual dessert. For a more sophisticated dish, try Almond-stuffed Medjool Dates, which are steeped in cinnamon and brandy.

BANANAS WITH MAPLE SYRUP & PECANS

½ cup coarsely chopped pecans
6 tablespoons maple syrup
4 bananas
Vanilla or rum-and-raisin ice cream, to serve

Place the chopped pecans and maple syrup in a small saucepan and set aside until required.

Cook the whole bananas in their skins on a prepared grill for 12-15 minutes, until the skins are completely black and the bananas are soft.

Just before serving, gently warm the pecans and maple syrup. To serve, remove the bananas from their skins and top with the warm nutty syrup and scoops of ice cream.
SERVES 4

FRUIT SKEWERS WITH CHOCOLATE-NUT SAUCE

12 strawberries
6 apricots, halved
3 pears, peeled and cut into quarters
2 tablespoons superfine sugar
6 wooden or metal skewers

CHOCOLATE-NUT SAUCE

4 ounces milk chocolate, chopped
⅔ cup light cream
6 marshmallows, chopped
¼ cup toasted and chopped skinless hazelnuts

Make the sauce by melting the chocolate, cream and marshmallows gently, stirring constantly. Then whisk to produce a smooth sauce and boil for 2 minutes to thicken. Stir in the nuts, and set the sauce aside.

Place the fruit in a bowl, sprinkle over the superfine sugar, and toss gently to coat. Divide the fruit between the skewers.

Place the fruit skewers on a prepared grill and cook them for 5-6 minutes, turning frequently, until the fruit is warmed through. Serve the skewers at once with the Chocolate-Nut Sauce passed separately for dipping.
SERVES 6

RIGHT: Fruit Skewers with Chocolate-Nut Sauce

EXOTIC FRUIT WITH PASSION FRUIT DIP

1 small ripe papaya, cut into 4 thick slices with
seeds removed
1 small ripe mango, cut into quarters around the pit
2 bananas, unpeeled and halved lengthwise
2 thick slices pineapple, halved
4 tablespoons melted unsalted butter
2 teaspoons sifted confectioner's sugar

PASSION FRUIT DIP
1 cup crème fraîche
1 tablespoon sifted confectioner's sugar
Pulp and juice of 3 passion fruit
Mint sprigs, to decorate

Mix the ingredients for the dip together in a bowl. Cover and refrigerate until required.

Place all the fruit on a large tray. Mix together the melted butter and confectioner's sugar, and brush the mixture all over the fruit. Cook all the fruit on a prepared grill, turning the papaya, mango and pineapple over occasionally until they begin to caramelize. The mango, pineapple and bananas will take about 6 minutes to cook, and the papaya about 4 minutes. Garnish with mint and serve the fruit with the dip.

SERVES 4

PEACH & ALMOND DESSERT WITH AMARETTO

1½ cups crumbled Madeira cake or pound cake
6 amaretti macaroon cookies, coarsely crushed
4 tablespoons Amaretto liqueur
4 ripe peaches, halved with pits removed
¼ cup toasted slivered almonds
½ cup freshly squeezed orange juice
Mascarpone cheese, to serve

Mix the Madeira cake, amaretti cookies and half the Amaretto liqueur together in a bowl. Divide the mixture between the hollows of the peaches. Sprinkle a few slivered almonds onto each peach half.

Mix the remaining Amaretto liqueur and the orange juice together. Place two peach halves on a large piece of foil. Spoon over one-quarter of the orange juice mixture and fold over the foil securely. Repeat with the remaining peaches to produce four foil packages.

Cook the foil-wrapped peaches on a prepared grill for about 10 minutes, until they are tender and warmed through. Serve with mascarpone cheese.

SERVES 4

TOP: Peach & Almond Dessert with Amaretto
BOTTOM: Exotic Fruit with Passion Fruit Dip

ALMOND-STUFFED MEDJOOL DATES

12 large fresh Medjool dates
¾ cup toasted blanched almonds
2 tablespoons mascarpone cheese or cream cheese
4 tablespoons brandy
2 cinnamon sticks, broken in half
2 tablespoons brown sugar
4 tablespoons freshly squeezed orange juice
Greek yogurt, to serve (optional)

Make a slit in the side of each date and remove and discard the pits.

Reserve 12 whole blanched almonds and chop the rest finely. Place them in a bowl and add the mascarpone cheese and half the brandy. Mix well to combine and fill the dates with the mixture, adding a whole almond to each cavity.

Place six dates on a large piece of foil and place a cinnamon stick on the foil with the dates. Mix the remaining brandy, brown sugar and orange juice together. Spoon half of the mixture over the dates. Wrap up the foil securely. Repeat with the remaining dates, cinnamon and orange juice mixture.

Cook the foil-wrapped dates on a prepared grill for about 10 minutes, until the dates are tender and warmed through. Serve with yogurt, if desired.

SERVES 4

TAMARILLOS WITH BROWN SUGAR

4 ripe tamarillos (tree tomatoes)
3 tablespoons Demerara sugar
Vanilla ice cream, to serve

Halve the tamarillos and place two halves on a piece of foil. Sprinkle with one-quarter of the Demerara sugar and fold the foil over securely to close. Repeat with the remaining tamarillos and sugar to produce four individual foil packages.

Cook the foil-wrapped tamarillos on a prepared grill for about 10 minutes, until they are warmed through and the sugar has melted. Serve at once with scoops of vanilla ice cream.

SERVES 4

TOP LEFT: Tamarillos with Brown Sugar
BOTTOM: Almond-stuffed Medjool Dates

ACCOMPANIMENTS

The collection of recipes in this chapter will help you provide a complete barbecue meal. Some of the accompaniments, such as Skewered New Potatoes and Olive, Basil & Parmesan Ciabatta, are actually cooked on the grill. Other recipes include rice and salad dishes, muffins and the classic Chili Beans. Although these are not cooked on the grill, they are quick and easy to prepare and make good accompaniments to many of the recipes in the book.

JASMINE & SESAME RICE

1 cup Thai jasmine rice or fragrant rice
1 teaspoon sesame oil
2 tablespoons toasted sesame seeds
4 scallions, finely chopped
4 tablespoons chopped fresh cilantro
2 teaspoons lime juice
Salt and ground black pepper

Cook the rice in boiling, salted water for about 10 minutes, or until it is tender. Drain and transfer the rice to a large bowl.

Add the remaining ingredients to the warm rice and stir gently to mix. Taste and adjust seasoning, if necessary, and serve at once. SERVES 4

SPICY RICE

1 cup mixed wild and long-grain rice
3 tablespoons olive oil
3 cloves garlic, crushed
1 teaspoon dried chili flakes
3 tablespoons chopped fresh parsley
¾ cup canned corn kernels
Salt and ground black pepper

Cook the rice in boiling, salted water for about 10 minutes, or until the rice is tender. Drain and set it aside. Heat the oil in a saucepan and cook the garlic for 2 minutes. Add the chili flakes and cook for a further 30 seconds. Stir the rice into the cooked garlic and chili, along with the parsley, corn and seasoning.
SERVES 4

RICE & PEAS

2 tablespoons vegetable oil
1 onion, thinly sliced
½ cup coconut cream, dissolved in
2¾ cups boiling water
2¾ cups vegetable stock
1½ cups long-grain rice
1 fresh red chili, seeded and finely chopped
2 tablespoons chopped fresh thyme
Salt and ground black pepper
¾ cup canned red kidney beans
1 tablespoon toasted shredded coconut, to garnish
Thyme sprigs, to garnish

Heat the oil in a saucepan, add the onion, and sauté for 5 minutes until golden. Add the coconut with its water, the stock, rice, chili, thyme and seasoning to the pan. Cover the pan and simmer for 20 minutes, until the rice grains have swelled and most of the liquid has been absorbed.

Uncover the pan, stir the kidney beans into the rice, and cook for a further 8-10 minutes, until the rice is tender and all the liquid has been absorbed. Garnish with toasted coconut and thyme, and serve at once.
SERVES 6

TOP: Jasmine & Sesame Rice
BOTTOM: Rice & Peas

CHILI BEANS

3 tablespoons vegetable oil
1 medium onion, chopped
2 cloves garlic, crushed
2-3 teaspoons hot chili powder
1 teaspoon cumin seeds
14-ounce can chopped tomatoes
⅔ cup red wine
2 tablespoons tomato paste
4 teaspoons molasses
2¼ cups canned red kidney beans
2¼ cups canned black-eyed peas
⅔ cup water
Salt and ground black pepper
3 tablespoons chopped fresh oregano

Heat the oil in a large saucepan, add the onion and garlic, and sauté for 3 minutes. Stir in the chili and cumin, and cook for a further minute.

Add the chopped tomatoes, wine, tomato paste and molasses, and simmer for 10 minutes. Add the two types of beans and the water. Season the beans, cover, and cook for a further 20 minutes. Stir in the oregano, taste and adjust seasoning, if necessary, and cook for a further 4-5 minutes. Serve the chili beans hot as an accompaniment to barbecued potatoes, burgers or frankfurters. SERVES 6

SKEWERED NEW POTATOES

32 baby new potatoes, about 1½ pounds in
total weight
4 tablespoons olive oil
Sea salt and ground black pepper
8 wooden skewers, soaked in cold water for
2 hours

HERB BUTTER
6 tablespoons softened butter
2 tablespoons chopped fresh herbs of your choice
Salt and ground black pepper

Scrub the potatoes and cook them in boiling, salted water for about 12 minutes, or until tender.

Drain the potatoes and, while they are still warm, toss with the olive oil and plenty of salt and pepper. Thread four potatoes onto each skewer and set aside until required.

Mix the ingredients for the Herb Butter together. Place the butter in an oblong shape on a piece of parchment paper or plastic wrap, and roll up to produce a cylinder. Refrigerate the butter until it becomes firm enough to slice.

Cook the potatoes on a prepared grill for 12-15 minutes, turning them frequently. Serve hot with the Herb Butter. SERVES 8

RIGHT: Chili Beans

ROASTED PEPPER & PASTA SALAD

6 ounces dried pasta shapes
4 halves sun-dried tomatoes in oil, drained and sliced
1 yellow bell pepper, broiled, skinned and sliced into strips
1 red bell pepper, broiled, skinned and sliced into strips
1 tablespoon chopped fresh oregano
1 tablespoon chopped fresh thyme

TAPENADE DRESSING

3 tablespoons extra virgin olive oil
1 tablespoon balsamic vinegar
1 clove garlic, crushed
1 teaspoon black olive tapenade
Salt and ground black pepper

Place the ingredients for the dressing in a screw-topped jar and shake well to combine. Taste and adjust seasoning, if necessary. Set aside until required.

Cook the pasta in boiling, salted water for 12-15 minutes, until it is tender. Drain and transfer the pasta to a large bowl. Pour the dressing over and add the remaining ingredients. Toss to combine. If time permits, let the salad stand for 1 hour before serving to allow the flavors to develop. SERVES 4

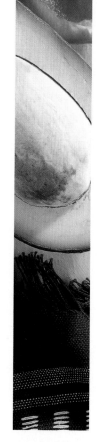

CRISP GREEN SALAD

2½ cups torn crisp lettuce leaves, such as Romaine, iceberg and curly endive
2 stalks celery, sliced on the diagonal
1 small avocado, peeled, pitted and chopped
2 scallions, sliced
¾ cup chopped cucumber
½ cup toasted cashews

CASHEW DRESSING

¾ cup toasted cashews
6 tablespoons sunflower oil
3 tablespoons cider vinegar
½ teaspoon brown sugar
Salt and ground black pepper

Make the dressing. Place the cashews in a food processor and grind coarsely. Add the oil, vinegar, brown sugar and seasoning, and blend briefly to produce a thick, nutty dressing.

Place the prepared salad ingredients in a large bowl. Just before serving, pour the dressing over and toss gently to combine. Serve at once. SERVES 4-6

TOP: Crisp Green Salad
BOTTOM: Roasted Pepper & Pasta Salad

CORNMEAL MUFFINS

1 cup coarse cornmeal
¾ cup self-rising flour
1 teaspoon baking powder
Pinch of salt
4 tablespoons butter
⅔ cup milk
1 large beaten egg
Butter for greasing

Preheat the oven to 400°F. Sift together the cornmeal, flour, baking powder and salt. Melt the butter in a small pan, and stir the milk and beaten egg into the melted butter.

Make a well in the center of the sifted dry ingredients. Pour in the liquid mixture and beat together to produce a smooth batter.

Grease an eight-cup muffin pan and divide the mixture between the cups. Bake in the oven for 18-20 minutes, until risen and golden. Let the muffins cool in the pan before removing them. MAKES 8 MUFFINS

BASIL AND PARMESAN MUFFINS

Add 16 chopped green olives, 12 coarsely chopped basil leaves and 4 tablespoons grated Parmesan cheese to the prepared muffin batter. Sprinkle 2 tablespoons grated Parmesan over the muffins once they are in the pan, and bake as described in the main recipe.

HERB MUFFINS

Add 4 tablespoons chopped fresh herbs of your choice to the prepared muffin batter, then bake as described in the main recipe.

CHEESE MUFFINS

Add ½ cup grated Gruyère cheese to the prepared muffin batter. Spoon the mixture into the pan and sprinkle with an additional ½ cup grated Gruyère. Bake as described in the main recipe.

OLIVE, BASIL & PARMESAN CIABATTA

1 loaf ciabatta bread
½ cup softened butter
6 stuffed green olives, finely chopped
6 tablespoons grated Parmesan cheese
10 large basil leaves, torn
Salt and ground black pepper

Cut slices in the ciabatta loaf, cutting almost through to the base. Mix the butter, olives, Parmesan, basil and salt and pepper together. Spread the flavored butter liberally on the cut slices of the ciabatta. Wrap the loaf in foil and place it on one side of a prepared grill for 20-30 minutes, until the butter has melted and the bread is hot. Serve at once. MAKES 1 LOAF

GARLIC & SUN-DRIED TOMATO CIABATTA

1 loaf ciabatta bread
½ cup softened butter
4 teaspoons sun-dried tomato paste
1 teaspoon fennel seeds
2 large cloves garlic, crushed
Salt and ground black pepper

Cut slices in the ciabatta loaf, as described in the recipe above. Mix the remaining ingredients together, then prepare and cook the bread as described above.

MAKES 1 LOAF

TOP: Cornmeal Muffins
BOTTOM: Garlic & Sun-dried Tomato Ciabatta

INDEX